You who are
The Bright and Morning Star
Come in radiant splendor
And flood each shadowed crevice
Of my sullen heart
Until the world shall know
I've touched a Star.

Tell Me Again, Lord, I Forget

RUTH HARMS CALKIN

LIVING BOOKS
Tyndale House Publishers, Inc.
Wheaton, Illinois

Second printing, Living Books edition, May 1986
Library of Congress Catalog Card Number 85-50813
ISBN 0-8423-6990-2
Copyright 1974 by Ruth Harms Calkin
All rights reserved
Printed in the United States of America

To my husband

ROLLIN

forever loving,

forever loved

CONTENTS

Myself and Others

TWO CHILDREN LEARNING

Today she came for a lesson—
A dear little girl
With a trace of impatience
Salting her words:

"I don't like these exercises.
I want to play beautiful music."

I've said this to You.

I said to her then
"This is the way to learn
Beautiful music.
I am your teacher—
Trust me and see."

Lord, I thought of the times
You've said this to me.

LITTLE KIDS

Eight years old
Blue eyes
Freckles
Pitcher on his team.
Yesterday he threw a rock
Which broke a window.
When I asked why, he blurted
"Because I'm just a little kid."

Reprimand
Tears
Reassured love . . .
And all the while
I was thinking, Lord
That with all our sophistication
And pretended poise
We're still just little kids.

We whimper and whine
Wail and throw tantrums
We excuse our intolerance
And ignore our responsibility
Toward other little kids.
We throw mud
Call names
Sulk in corners
And murmur against discipline.

We're little kids
With the nature of sin
Hopelessly trying to bandage
Our own broken hearts.
There's a road to maturity
Which starts at the Cross
But too often we look for a detour—
A shortcut to Heaven.

Remind me of this often, Lord
Between broken windows
Black eyes
And poor report cards.

I WEEP WITH THE JOY
OF MY LOVE

Lord, I weep with the joy
Of my love for him . . .

He seldom walks in
He darts—
Arms outstretched
For a vigorous hug.
He's seldom alone
A Little Leaguer trails him—
Three feet tall
Four teeth missing.
(A dog named Tagalong tags along.)
He's seldom hungry
He's starved.
"David and me would like some cookies."
"You mean 'David and I.' "
"Sure, Mom, you too."
He seldom runs out to play
He races.
At the table he seldom swallows
He inhales.
At bedtime he seldom prays
He climbs up on God's lap
And in a manner most beautiful
He whispers his own private secrets.
He seldom asks
He thanks—

For this and this
And especially for this . . .
He seldom sleeps—
With a cloud for a wagon
He hitches to a star
Then he rides on the moon
Until dawn.

Lord, I weep with the joy
Of my love for him . . .

VERY PERSONAL

Wherever we are
The pressure of
My husband's hand
Brings my own answering pressure.
We always know.

Lord
May the pressure
Of Your Love
Bring my answering pressure.
May we always know.

ETERNAL TRAGEDY

She rushed to my arms
With eight-year-old candor
Broken heart
Tears.

Mary didn't pass—
We won't be together next year.
Fourth-grade tragedy
Separated friends. . . .

Here in our town
There are countless Marys
Countless Joes
Who may never pass
From death unto life.
Eternal tragedy
Separated families.

Lord
Does my heart break?
Have I shed a single tear?

ANSWERED LETTER

Lord
In answer to her letter
I've written what I felt
You wanted me to say.
Now may my words of advice
Stand the scrutiny
Of my own conscience.

DON'T ANSWER

I am able, I find
To express my thoughts
Quite articulately
When making a criticism.

Why in the world
Do I humiliate myself
With such ridiculous
Stuttering and stammering
When making an apology?

Lord, I'm not really sure
I want You to answer.

PROOF, LORD?

At the promotion dinner
I happened to sit next to a preacher
Who told me
He had the most alive church in town.
To prove it
He showed me his date book.

WALKING TOGETHER

It would be sheer mockery, Lord
It would be subtle hypocrisy
For me to kneel
Anguished and weeping
Before Your Cross
Unless—

As I walk with You now
Down my personal Emmaus Road
I introduce You
With singing joy
To the broken and bound
The weary and worn
The depressed and defeated
Whom we meet on the way.

And, Lord, I observe
That as we walk together
Foot traffic thickens.

LOVING ME AS YOU DO

When my rapport with You
Is disturbed, Lord
My rapport with myself
Is utterly destroyed.

I am irritable
Little things get in my way
I am short with my family
The house is too small
My neighbors bore me
The phone frustrates me
Feelings of guilt gnaw at me.
Just leave me alone, I scream
I'll do it myself.

But You patiently wait to be gracious.
You gently nudge me to attention.
For knowing me as You do
Loving me as You do
You understand so well
That when I want You least
I need You most.

I WONDER

You know, Lord, how I serve You
With great emotional fervor
In the limelight.
You know how eagerly I speak for You
At a women's club.
You know how I effervesce when I promote
A fellowship group.
You know my genuine enthusiasm
At a Bible study.

But how would I react, I wonder
If You pointed to a basin of water
And asked me to wash the calloused feet
Of a bent and wrinkled old woman
Day after day
Month after month
In a room where nobody saw
And nobody knew.

THE LETTER

Lord, my heart aches
Remembering how he sat there
In his dimly lit kitchen
Warming his shivering spirit
With a cup of hot tea.
I couldn't help but notice
The weary lines
Etching his rugged face—
His lonely eyes.
In his trembling hand
He clutched a pencil—
Just a stub of pencil, Lord
And when he heard my step
He pointed to the letter
On the table
Bravely finished before I came.
Not a letter, really—
Just a note
Expressing all he needed to convey.
"Dear Son:
Mother has passed away" . . .
For over sixty years
He walked with her
Through clear and stormy weather.
Now grant to him, I pray
The grace to walk alone
With deep repose
Until that bright and shining dawn
When You shall say
"You're home."

SENSITIZE ME, LORD

I spoke to her at the bus stop
But she turned the other way.
My immediate reaction:
A rush of resentment—
She's ignoring me
She doesn't really like me
I've always suspected it
Now I know.

Suddenly she looked toward me
Startled, but sincere:
"Forgive me—I didn't see you."
(Until then I hadn't noticed
The agony lining her face.)
A hesitant pause
A catch in her voice—
"I just came from the doctor's office,
Our little boy has leukemia.
It's all a terrible nightmare."

Lord, Lord
What loathsome selfishness.
A mother stricken with grief
Her heart soaked with pain
An hour of black catastrophe
And I thought only of me.
Cleanse me, Lord
Sensitize me
Until my first concern is for others
And my last concern is for me.

AUXILIARY MEETING

Lord
In an impulsive moment
I offered our home
For the next Auxiliary meeting.
Now I'm terribly reticent
I want very much to back out.
I can't imagine
What I was thinking—
All those women
With their hilltop homes
Their expensive furniture
Their elaborate motifs
Just picture them, Lord
Huddled together
In our small living room.
Doesn't it seem ridiculous?
But, Lord
You always see beyond
My flimsy excuses.
Once again You jolt me
With a sudden reminder:
I need never apologize for a home
In which You delight to live.
What shall I serve for refreshments, Lord?

BUSY BUSY BUSY

My dear, frenzied friend—
How I ache for her, Lord.
I just can't believe
How busy she is.

She eats so fast
Scolds so loud
Clings so tight
Complains so bitterly
Worries so intensely
Rushes so wildly
Shops so impulsively
Plans so fearfully
Panics so frequently
Shatters so utterly

No wonder she insists
There's no time to pray.

FOREVER TOGETHER

Riding home from the cemetery
Tears still flooding my heart
I glanced at a billboard and read
Families who pray together
Stay together.

Oh, yes, Lord—
Through all Eternity.

FRAGRANCE

Lord
If like a fragile flower
Torn petal by petal
My heart must continue to tear
Let there be fragrance.

HOSPITAL PATIENTS

Do they ever get used to it, Lord?
The narrow hospital beds
The walls of confinement
The monotony
The aching fatigue?
Do they ever get used
To dragging hours of surging pain
Day after day of shadowed loneliness
Night after night of silent sobs?
Oh, Lord
What defenseless lack of fulfillment.
Do they ever get used to it?
Lord, do You?

POOR REHEARSAL

Last Saturday morning, Lord
I rehearsed my troubles
To my next-door neighbor
As though I had come
To the end of my rope.
Perhaps if I had rehearsed
Your great goodness instead
My neighbor would have
Looked less puzzled
When I left for church on Sunday.
Please change my rehearsal tones.

MOVING DAY

Lord
Day after day
For twenty years
I joyfully thanked You
For our family of six
Living harmoniously
In our comfortable home.
Today, dear Lord
I joyfully thank You
For our family of five
And for a thousand
Beautiful memories
Of one who so quietly moved
To the home You prepared
And now lives in splendor
With You.

I AM LEARNING

Lord, I am learning

That marriage from first to last
Is an adventure—
A long series of recurring "happenings"
In which we triumph or fail.

That when I let God be God
When according to Your Word
I joyfully submit
To my husband's authority
My sense of fulfillment
Is at high peak.

I can face life head-on
I can live with myself creatively—
Not ironclad rules
But ironclad love.
It works, Lord
Just as You said it would.

I am learning.

THE SEMINAR

Lord, this seminar I'm attending
Is extremely stimulating.
Response to fresh insight
Is always electrifying.
The discussion this morning
Included the question—
"If you could choose
To be somebody else
Who would you choose to be?"

A challenging question, Lord
But today my personal contribution
Was noticeably nil.
Today I simply observed.
After all—
If I suddenly chose
To be somebody else
How would You complete
Your Plan for me?

TOUGH ONE

Lord
Help me to be her friend—
To care for her genuinely
Without envy shrinking my heart.
When I see her at the banquet tonight
Poised
Radiant
Beautifully attired
May I congratulate her
With honest enthusiasm
Regardless of the fact
That both our husbands
Were eligible for promotion
And hers won.

WHAT'S WRONG WITH ME?

What's wrong with me, Lord?

Week after week
I begged You to take her.
In agony I wept and waited
While she grappled
With insidious pain.
I watched the gradual decline
Of her once strong and lovely body.
I saw her lines of weariness
Her constant discomfort.
I listened to her broken sobs
As she pleaded for release.
I felt the pressure
Of her trembling fingers
When the gripping pain intensified.
I sensed her growing weakness
Her deep depression.
Through sleepless nights
I listened to her labored breathing.
In the darkness I cried to You—
Over and over I cried. . . .

Then yesterday morning, Lord
At the first streak of dawn
You answered my prayer.
Gently You took her to Yourself
You rewarded her with fullness of joy.
Thank You, Lord.

Yet even while I thank You
I wish I could have kept her
Just one more day.

What's wrong with me?

IT'S GOING JUST FINE

Five minutes ago, Lord
Our phone rang.
When I heard my husband's voice
I felt an unexpected rush of joy.
He said: "I've been praying for you—
How's it going?"
Oh, Lord
It's going just fine.
After thirty-eight years
Wonderfully fulfilling
Joyfully expanding
It's going just fine.
Dreaming and scheming
Exchanging opinions
Expressing convictions . . .
Hurting and forgiving
Arms holding
Hearts healing . . .
Fearing and praying
Shielding through sorrow
Embracing through tears . . .
Investing and risking
Facing the darkness
Waiting for dawn . . .
Yearning and searching
Climbing a mountain
Stretching for stars . . .
Grateful
Eternally grateful
To God who patterned it all . . .
See what I mean, Lord?
It's going just fine.

THE QUARREL

Oh, Lord
It was a foolish quarrel.
Hasty words
Guarded glances
Phantoms of anger and self-pity.

I was wrong
He was wrong
We each knew.

Still our clashing wills
Thrust a wall against the sky
Tall and obstinate—
As immovable as our stubborn pride.
Then all at once
His words came spilling
Like cool spring water
Over jagged rocks:
"Love like ours
Is much too big for this.
Forgive me . . .
Please forgive me."
Sheltered in his arms
I remembered, Lord—

As faith can move a mountain
So love removes a wall.

PROMISE KEPT

Lord
Years ago on our wedding day
We promised never to say good-night
With anger still hovering—
Never to turn our backs
Hurling bitter words.
But, Lord, must *I* always be the one to yield?
Are personal opinions out, for me?
Am I some kind of mechanical robot
Simply because I bear the title wife?

I'm sorry, Lord . . .
We both know I'm handcuffed with self-pity
Because I lost last night's argument.
In spite of moments of wrangling
Moments of competitive rivalry
Thank You again for a marriage
Consistently fulfilling
Year after beautiful year.
Teach us both
To express without exploding
To persuade without pouting
To disagree without being disagreeable.

And may we sleep well.

LATER, LORD

Lord, in the depth of my being
I want to be free . . .
So free that every allegiance
That tends to push You
Into the background
Will shatter to dust.
So free that I shall stand utterly loyal
In the midst of a hissing crowd.
So free that I shall not rebel
When You alter my personal preferences.
So free that I shall yield all my tomorrows
To Your sovereign control.
So free that I shall seek You persistently
And follow You exclusively.
But, Lord
When You ask "How soon?"
My heart winces.
May I think about it
A little while?

PLEASE LISTEN TO ME

Lord, I'm terribly ashamed.
All day long I've flung my childish complaints
Like a schoolboy throwing paper darts.
I've overstuffed each whimpering monologue
With endless references to
Me myself and I.
Not once did I give You a side glance
Or a chance to get a word in edgewise.
Then tonight after dinner
My husband suddenly stopped me short.
Hungry for communication
He pleadingly urged—
"Please listen to me . . .
Just listen to me."
Startled, but grateful
I faced him directly
And quietly listened.
I knew at that moment, Lord
The pleading was his
But the message was Yours.

Seasonal
Minimoods

EASTER MORN

It was early dawn, Lord
And I was looking for You.
Looking
Looking
And weeping.
Within the dismal tomb
I searched
I called
I waited
But nowhere could I find You.

Then through the gray
There came a vibrant voice:
He's risen!
He's alive!
Rush toward joy!
You'll find Him everywhere
Outside the tomb—
But never, *never* there.

Startled and amazed
I left the tomb
To walk the path of praise—
Then looking up
I saw You by my side
And all of life became
An Easter morn.

FATHER'S DAY

Many a time we visit them, Lord:
The sick, the aged, the senile.
It's the courteous thing to do
The decent thing.
In hospitals and homes
We sing our well-worn songs
Quote mechanically the 23rd Psalm
And pat bony shoulders.
On and on we chatter
Cheerfully, of course
(Often patronizingly).
We seldom listen attentively
But somehow we always pray:
"Thank You for these dear saints,
Bless their fading years . . ."
Then, Lord
At the first convenient moment
We hustle down the long corridor
Eager to gulp fresh air again.

It's different today, Lord
Drastically different.
Today I'm visiting my dad
And that represents my family.
Today I face reality
In a clashing, inescapable way.

My dad:
Once virile, strong, alert
Once intellectually stimulating
A scholar, a teacher
Who dreamed noble dreams
And planned lavish schemes.
From the pulpit he challenged youths
Comforted the oppressed
And boldly presented the claims of Christ.
He loved and laughed and lived.

Forgive my glibness, Lord
My indifference
My condescension.
Create in me a deep compassion
A tender empathy.
In every ward and room
May I see a dad
A mother
A person of infinite worth.
Above all
With every gentle touch
May I see You.

BACCALAUREATE

Lord
The baccalaureate speaker
Was tremendous—
Poised
Polished
And extremely handsome.
He captivated the seniors
With his emphatic thrust:
"Living is a thing you do
Now or never."

I kept wishing he'd say
"Living is a thing you do
Forever."

FOURTH OF JULY

I was thinking, Lord—
Our Fourth of July pattern
Seldom varies:
Hot humid air
Hamburger fry
Tender corn
Fresh strawberry ice cream
Then finally
Those traditional sparklers
When darkness tiptoes in.

Funny thing about sparklers—
We never tire of their
Noiseless beauty . . .
Lord, now that I have signed
My Declaration of Dependence
Make me Your sparkler
Noiseless
But beautiful
Especially in the dark.

THANKSGIVING MORNING

Early on Thanksgiving morning
Before my family awakened
I began to form a list entitled
Reasons for Gratitude.
Then, halfway down the page
I pensively wondered—
Lord, do I give You any reasons
To be thankful for me?

THE GIFT

It's Christmas, Lord
It's Your birthday.
What can I give You—
You who have given
So much to me?
I search and search
Through my talents
My possessions
My friendships
My loves
But with all my searching
I find nothing new.
Strangely—
Whatever I could offer
Is always that
Which You have first
Given me.
And now in the soft silence
I hear You say
What I want from you—
Is you.

CHRISTMAS

The stable—my heart
The guiding star—Your perfect plan
The Song—"Just As I Am"
The gift—my irrevocable Yes
The joy—Your immeasurable love
The hope—the King is coming
Lord
This is my personal paraphrase
Of Christmas.

WEDDING ANNIVERSARY

Lord
Today is our wedding anniversary
Thank You for the exquisite gift
Of love fulfilled.
You have made our marriage
What it was meant to be—
A dynamic demonstration
Of caring and sharing
Of giving and living.

When we invited You
To our wedding
That warm September day
(I still remember the blue blue sky)
Did You plan our joy then—
Or did You wait
Until You moved in with us?

SATURDAYS

I love Saturdays, Lord—
Our very own day
For freedom and fun.
On Saturdays
We sleep an hour longer
Drink steaming coffee in bed
Fix waffles for breakfast
And climb our private hill
Holding hands.
Sometimes I wish every day
Were Saturday
But then
Maybe we wouldn't
Feel so free
Or laugh so much
Or climb our hill
Holding hands.
Let's keep it like it is.
Thank You, Lord
For Saturdays.

JANUARY

It's January, Lord—
The drab, dreary middle—
And my thoughts are as drab
As the miserable month.
Does everybody hit a January slump
Or am I the only one?
The first week wasn't too bad:
There were Christmas thank-yous to write
A few resolutions to store away
The huddle of year-end sales.
But thank-you notes bring no returns
And resolutions are quickly broken
And marked-down trinkets fast lose appeal.
When You said
Behold, I make all things new
Did You forget January, Lord?
Or in January do *I* sometimes forget You?

Common
Things

BEAUTIFUL BELONGING

Before I knew You, Lord
It was terribly important
To flaunt my culinary art
With a moist and tender roast.
Now that I'm Yours
It is far more important
To serve Your gentleness
To our guests.

Before I knew You
It was terribly important
To snatch every weed
From our meticulous yard.
Now that I'm Yours
It is far more important
To express neighborly concern
Over the back fence.

Before I knew You
It was terribly important
To check the television schedule
From night to night.
Now that I'm Yours
It is far more important
To check Your plan
From day to day.

What an incredible change—
This Beautiful Belonging!

I DO GET HUNGRY

Lord, it could very well happen
That I'll be fired
Before I'm permanently hired.
After all, it's been years
Since I've worked in an office.
I'm rusty at taking dictation.
My typing has degenerated
To the hunt and peck system.
I'm slow as a snail
On documentary reports.
These intricate machines turn me off
Before I grasp how to turn them on.
My boss is courteous, but demanding.
I have a feeling he's biting his tongue
While biding his time.
Any day now I expect to be called in
To be called down.
When it happens, Lord
When he hands me my severance check
Give me the grace
To hold back the tears.
Then stuff my knapsack
With a new brand of courage
As once again I trudge the streets
Seeking employment.
As You undoubtedly know—
I don't have an Elijah
And I do get hungry.

JOHN 15:5

Lord
Often You come in the nick of time
Before I collide with a crisis—

Yesterday
There I was
Rushing
Dashing madly
Company coming for dinner
The table unset
The salad half made
My hair in wild hysteria
And You interrupted
With Your quiet plea:
"Let Me help you."

It was better after that, Lord—
From boil to simmer
Far less hectic
My head stayed on.
Just one more incident
To prove I can't do anything
Without You.

You said so first.

PERFECT MATCH

Thank You, dear Lord
For shopping with me.
You helped me find a red bag
To match my red shoes.
Then, just as we left the store
You startled me by asking:
Are you always as eager
To match your will with Mine?
Sometimes it is easier
To match red with red.

REFRESHED

Lord, I laugh with delight
When I think of the common things
You use to prove Your Presence!
This noon, for example:
There I stood in the kitchen
Washing a head of lettuce
Pulling the leaves one by one
To get to the heart—
And suddenly, clear as a bell
I heard You say
The closer you get to My heart
The more satisfying it is . . .
And I was refreshed
But not from the lettuce.

NEW HOME

Lord, thank You
Oh, thank You for our new home
Fresh and clean and glistening.
Even the walls smile, Lord
As we walk from room to room.
We feel alive
So blessedly peaceful here
As if You had given us
A brand new beginning.
Now, Lord
As we adjust to our new surroundings
Our new neighbors
Even our new shopping center
Give us a fresh concept
Of what it means
To adjust to each other.
May we remember
We are persons created
In Your image
For Your divine purpose
Always in the process of becoming.
Remind us often
That we belong to You
Before we belong to each other.
Lord
You who make all things new
Make our marriage as fresh and exciting
As our new home.
May we anticipate joy
As our new tulip bulbs
Anticipate spring.

LORD, WILL I EVER LEARN?

You saw the whole scene, Lord.
Congested traffic
Conglomerate thoughts
Choking smog
Nerves jarring.
You know how he infuriated me
Selfish driver
Egotistical.
He insisted on changing lanes, Lord
Recklessly cutting in
Stopping short
Carelessly oblivious.
Then at a signal I watched it happen:
Sputtering motor
Smoke billowing
Radiator pouring water
Stymied driver.

With forced control
Plus an open smirk
(Sorry, Lord)
I managed to maneuver around him.
Two miles from home
Spontaneous relief.

Then just as I turned the corner
Your voice again:
I am
Much more patient
With you.

WHY?

Standing here
At the kitchen sink
My hands immersed
In soapsuds
All of a sudden I know
With fresh, penetrating force
I am only really whole
When I am wholly Yours.
Yet with proud self-assertion
I often choose to be
Incomplete.
Why, Lord?

MY PERSISTENT DESIRE

Lord of my years
My days
My moments
Make this my persistent desire:
To live to Your glory
To sing to Your praise
In the hidden valley
In the piercing noise of city streets
In the chaos of a shattered world
And where it is often most difficult—
In my yellow kitchen
Between the refrigerator
And the copper stove.

LADY IN PINK

Lord, it happened so unexpectedly
That October Sunday.
I caught a glimpse of her
Starting slowly down the aisle—
Silver hair
Pink shawl hugging her tiny frame.
Your prompting was inescapable . . .
Take her home for dinner.
Her eyes glistened with surprise:
"Nobody's invited me to dinner
Since Charlie died."

Lord, it was a rewarding Sunday.
She was like a happy child
Celebrating Christmas . . .
We talked about Charlie
About knitting and painting
About peach preserves
And the goodness of God.
Our home was charged with love—
With laughter.

And, Lord
We'll never forget her parting words:
"When I see Charlie someday
I'll tell him I had a corner of Heaven
One Sunday after church."

Thank You, Lord
For our dear lady in pink

And for making our home
A corner of Heaven.

THE STAB

Lord, I was thoroughly exasperated
With our newsboy.
Three times my husband requested
That he throw our paper on the porch
But there it was again—
In the middle of the lawn.
I dashed out the door
To vent my irritation.
In no uncertain terms I made it clear
That such negligence was inexcusable
That he'd never hold a responsible job
That most boys his age . . .

Well, Lord, You heard me—
Fury flying.
He looked at me curiously
Trying to put it together.
Then suddenly the dawn:
"Hey, I know you—
You're my sister's Sunday school teacher
You talk about God and love and stuff."
Lord, I'm stabbed with shame.
Forgive me
Recreate me
Until my life Monday
Authentically reflects
What I teach on Sunday.

MISGIVINGS

Tonight as I set our small table
His plate and my plate
Red napkins evenly folded
Quivering candle-glow—
I thought of his prayer of gratitude
Reverently expressed day after day:
"We're thankful for *this* meal, too."
Lord, in his voice I hear You.
In his smile I see You.
In his love I sense Your love.

No wonder I feel some misgivings
In serving plain vegetable stew.

INDELIBLE INK

I love her exuberance, Lord
Her refreshing spontaneity.
I smile when I think
How she rushed into the house
(Blue eyes aglow)
And thrust her new book
Into my hands:
"Please write my name on my book
In great big letters
So everybody knows
It belongs to me."

Yes, Lord
Yes.
I want that too.
Write Your name
On the chapters of my life—
My thoughts
Motives
Secret dreams . . .
Write Your name
On my total being
So everybody knows
I belong to You.

And, Lord
Indelible ink, please.

COINCIDENCES

Lord, I was intrigued
With the brilliant vocabulary
Of the patient sitting next to me
In the reception room.
I don't remember
The start of our conversation
But suddenly we were discussing prayer.
I shared rather freely
Your pertinent answers
To my day-by-day requests.

Labeling himself a skeptic
He smiled and said courteously
"What you consider answered prayer
I choose to call coincidence."
You know how it is with me, Lord—
I'm always slightly ill at ease
In the Big Middle
Of a theological discussion.
I'm much more at home in my kitchen
Mixing muffin batter
Or tossing green salads.
Frankly I was relieved
When the dentist called my name.
But one thing I do know, Lord
When I pray, "coincidences" happen.
When I don't pray they stop . . .

So thank You again and again
For ten thousand "coincidences"
Always in the nick of time
When I pray.

BUSY DAY

Lord, this is one of the days
I must ask You to preserve my sanity
In the midst of turmoil.
I'm so pressed by commitments—
Plus a thousand trivial tasks—
That I can scarcely see over my head.
So I plead for enough wisdom
To sort my priorities carefully.
Regardless of my frenzied schedule
May I keep my sense of humor
And even enjoy a hearty chuckle or two.

Calm my quivering nerves
With mental flashes from Your Word.
Help me to maintain
At least a semblance
Of Mary-Martha balance.
And tonight when we're together again
Should my husband confront me with
"What have you been doing today?"
May my answer be genuine and gentle:
"Part of the time, darling
I've thanked God for you."

MORNING STAR

You who are
The Bright and Morning Star
Come in radiant splendor
And flood each shadowed crevice
Of my sullen heart
Until the world shall know
I've touched a Star.

Discipleship

ANOTHER WORD FOR TRUSTING

Lord, I used to think
I could prove my trust in You
By refusing to fear.
Now I see that fear
Does not dissolve
With my timid command.
Far better to cling to You
While You rebuke the fear.

Clinging is another word
For trusting.

THE TASK

Lord, You give me a task
So utterly impossible
So totally beyond comprehension—
The very thought of it
Startles me.
I want to run hide escape
Anything, Lord.

Then You electrify me
You invade and permeate me
You penetrate every fiber of me
Until the task is accomplished
By Your own magnificent power.

Then You praise the performance
Your creativity achieved
And You reward me beyond expectation—
As though I had done it
All by myself.

My Father.

INSIGHT

While I was "praying," Lord
Demanding this
Insisting on that
You pierced me
With lightning-swift insight.

My bitter complaints
My self-centered whims
Do not constitute prayer
Just because they begin
"Dear God."

FEELING SPIRITUAL

Lord, I keep remembering
Our happy time last night—
Just You and me
In the quiet of our family room.
I had been reading a devotional book
Very "spiritual"
Very inspirational
So challenging
I doubted that I'd ever reach the goal.
Suddenly the book felt heavy
Sentences twirled
Words collided
And with all my valiant effort
I simply could not feel "spiritual."
Then, glancing at a Charlie Brown book
I thought I heard You say
"Let's read it together—
You and me."
I was delighted.
We read and laughed
And read and laughed . . .
And just as we finished the last page
You said what I needed most to hear:
"Never worry about feeling 'spiritual.'
Just share *everything* with me."

IN THE MORNING

". . . joy cometh in the morning" (Psalm 30)

Today, Lord
I have an unshakable conviction
A positive resolute assurance
That what You have spoken
Is unalterably true.

But today, Lord
My sick body feels stronger
And the stomping pain quietly subsides.
Tomorrow. . . .

And then tomorrow
If I must struggle again
With aching exhaustion
With twisting pain
Until I am breathless
Until I am utterly spent
Until fear eclipses the last vestige of hope
Then, Lord
Then grant me the enabling grace
To believe without feeling
To know without seeing
To clasp Your invisible hand
And wait with invincible trust

For the morning.

TEN TO ONE

Lord, I ask more questions
Than You ask.
The ratio, I would suppose
Is ten to one.

I ask:
Why do You permit this anguish?
How long can I endure it?
What possible purpose does it serve?
Have You forgotten to be gracious?
Have I wearied You?
Have I offended You?
Have You cast me off?
Where did I miss Your guidance?
When did I lose the way?
Do You see my utter despair?

You ask:
Are you trusting Me?

ERADICATION

Lord
I can no more
Eradicate my own guilt
Than I can
Sit on my own lap.
You alone can cleanse me.
While You accomplish the impossible
May I sit on Your lap?
Thank You for holding me, Lord.
I like it here.

YOU'RE IN MY WAY

This morning, Lord
I heard a distraught mother
Say to her lively son
"You're in my way—move."
This very same morning
You said to me
"You're in My way—stay."
How good it is
To be Your child.

LONGING TO PLEASE YOU

With all my heart, Lord
I long to please You.
But too often I lack wisdom
Or am shackled by indecision
Or deterred by incalculables.
Enable me, Lord
To relax in Your love
Released and radiantly confident
That my longing to please You
Pleases You most.

NO COMPROMISE

Walking home through fog and mist
Still pondering
Still puzzled and unsure
I desperately hoped we'd settle it.
That's why I said:
"When I *know* I'll *do*."

But You wouldn't drop it, Lord
Not for a minute.
In fact, Your response was firm:
"When you *do* you'll *know*."

Then with soft gentleness You asked:
"When did I fail you last?"

MISSING CHAPTER

Often, Lord
I feel achingly incomplete
Like the missing chapter
In a book.
But then I remember
You have not yet finished
The manuscript.
Forgive me
If I seem presumptuous
But have You set
A publication date?

DOUBLE EXPOSURE

Lord
Enable the woman in me
To smile with assurance
At the little girl in me
Who is still too afraid
Of ghosts and goblins.

I HAVE YOU

Sick depressed anxious
Fatigued frustrated
Puzzled perplexed lonely
Desperate despairing
Lord, for this I have You.

WHO WILL CLAP FOR ME?

I am often dramatic
Sometimes ecstatic
In the role I play
On the stage of Life.
I bow
And smile
And bask
In the limelight
Hoarding each moment
Of thunderous applause.
But when the curtain is pulled
For the last time
When the crowds have dispersed
And the stage is dark
Who will clap for me then, Lord?
You?

TIC-TAC-TOE

Sometimes, Lord
I get the impression
We're playing a game
Of tic-tac-toe.
I draw my X
You draw Your O.
Then just as I contemplate
The next move
You draw a straight line
Which finishes the game.
You always win, Lord
Always.
Is it because Your circle
Is Whole
Complete
Total
Like You?

HEARTSTRINGS

Lord, with no sense of direction
I'm forever losing my way.
Please tie a string
From Your heart to mine
So that even in the darkness
I'll feel the tug of Your heart
And find my way home.

BIG SWITCH

Once again I have utterly failed.
This time I thought I would make it.
I honestly thought I could cut it.
I thought it was all sewed up.
But here alone in my silent room
Your message rings loud and clear:
"Turn yourself in
And I will take over."
Could we make the Big Switch
Now, Lord?

IT'S YOUR MOVE

All through the long dreary hours
Of this rough toilsome day
I have struggled to believe
That Your plan is good
That the blows and bruises
Will stablish me
That the staggering changes
Will settle me.
I have struggled to believe
That Your way is perfect.

But waiting here alone
Shrouded in thick loneliness
I confess I don't see it.
Frankly I just don't see
That Your way is perfect.
And now I hear You say
I didn't say you would see it—
I only said—it is.
So, Lord, it's Your move.
Good-night.

THANK YOU FOR WAITING

Had You given in to me, Lord
On the thing I wanted so much
My life today
Would be a sorry mess.

I tell You nothing new—
I simply repeat
What You told me
Long, long ago.
Finally today I see it—
From Your point of view.
Thank You for not giving in to me.
Thank You most of all
For patiently waiting
For me to give in to You.

REAL PROBLEM

Lord
Your dedicated servant said:
"Never doubt in the darkness
What God tells you in the light."
I've got a real problem, Lord.
I doubt even in the light.

I'M DROWNING

Lord, I'm drowning
In a sea of perplexity.
Waves of confusion
Crash over me.
I'm too weak
To shout for help.
Either quiet the waves
Or lift me above them—
It's too late
To learn to swim.

THE CHOICE

Lord, You are indeed relentless:
You insist that my love be unrivaled
That my loyalty be uncompromising
That my surrender be irrevocable.
What do You want, Lord
Everything?
It's frightening.
Yet not as frightening
As staying as I am.

LIKE NOW

There are black and dismal times, Lord
When there is nothing and no one but You
When encouragement from friends
(However sincere and honest)
Rings shallow and repetitious
When books seem nothing more
Than jumbled sentences
When music depresses
When food is offensive
When sleep is evasive
There are such times, Lord

Like now.

AM I GROWING?

"Consider the lilies of the field
How they grow . . ."
Yes, Lord, I know
They grow *in the dark.*
Just now it is dark
Very dark, Lord.

Am I growing?

Just Me
and You,
Lord

THE REASON

Lord, we both know
I come to You
Boldly
Persistently
Expectantly
Day after day
Need after need
As if everything
In my entire life
Depended upon it.
There's a reason, Lord—
It does.

NOW YOU HAVE ME, GOD

Now You have me, God!
You have me irrevocably.
No reserve
No retreat
No turning back.

Now You have me, God!
All I feel
Dream
Aspire
All I long withheld.
My resistance
Triumphs
Defeats
My stalwart resolves
My crumbling dreams
My glittering awards
My blind alleys.

Now You have me, God!
All which is past
All which is now
All that may yet unfold.
The barriers are broken
The turmoil has stilled
Your Word is my Yes
Your notes are my song.

Now You have me, God!
You knocked
And still knocked
And I opened the door.
Now at last—
At long last
I know:

Joy!
As the rushing sea.
Peace!
As a meadow at twilight.
Strength!
As a towering mountain.
Trust!
As a wide-eyed child
Who walks
In the gentle rain
Holding
A father's hand.

MINIMOODS

You amaze me, Lord
Really, You amaze me.
Again and again
I bring You my minimoods:
Moods of depression
Resentment
Fear.
With every conceivable mood
I kneel in Your Presence
Sometimes impatiently
Often desperately
Always longingly.

And then—
In ways I cannot comprehend
Or possibly explain
I begin to sense
The pressure of You:
Melting
Molding
Transforming
Until minimoods of confusion
Become maximoments of silent joy.
It is too wonderful, Lord—
Much too wonderful.

Nothing is too hard for You
Not even me.

WHEN I AM WITH YOU

When I am with You, Lord
It is as though
I were given
A cup of cool water
Dipped from
An ever-flowing
Never-ceasing stream.
The water glistens
As a piece of clear ice
Tingles against
The side of my cup.
I want to drink
More
And more
And more
As though I could
Never drink enough—
And yet while I drink
I am satisfied
Completely.

What a strange and beautiful
Paradox!

PAINFUL

Lord
Too often my talents
Have been on display
For public inspection.
Now I am painfully learning
The only important thing:
Your reflection.

OPEN THY MOUTH WIDE

(Psalm 81:10)

You said it, Lord
You said it!
"Open thy mouth wide
And I will fill it."
I read with glowing heart
And growing love.
Never again will I
Shut my mouth
For You promised
A gold mine of blessing
If I open it wide.

DISCOVERY

Lord, I have discovered
That when I try
In simple ways
To be something to others
I utterly fail
Unless You are everything
To me.

MY DELIGHT

"You are My Delight . . ."
This, dear God
You said to Jesus
At the moment of His baptism
There in the River Jordan.
He is Your Son
I am Your child
Forever related to You through Him.

Baptize me, dear God
In the river of Your Love
Your Joy
Your Power
Until with deep and widening gladness
You can say to me
Your chosen child
"You are My delight."

MAKE YOURSELF AT HOME

With extreme joy, Lord
I offer my heart as Your home.
I have purposely left it unfurnished
Without lavish decor.
No plush carpeting
No velvet drapes
Not even an original oil
Or an engraved silver service.
Examine it first for cleanliness—
Every room
Every closet
Then furnish it according
To Your own magnificent taste.
The door is wide open—
Don't even bother to ring the bell.

A BETTER WAY

Lord, I'm utterly exhausted
From standing on tiptoe
Shouting my numerous wants.
My lips are dry
My eyes burn
My muscles ache
My nerves are tense.
I'm beginning to wonder
If it would be better
For me to relax
While You lean down
And whisper to me.

IMPATIENT

I know You want
To make me
More real within
Than the false lashes
And color
And polish
I wear without

But, Lord
It takes so long.

MOUNTAINS—MOLEHILLS

Oh, Lord
You've done it again
You've turned
My flimsy little tune
Into a swelling crescendo.
But that's the way You are—
Always making mountains
Out of our molehills of joy.

METHOD OF ACHIEVEMENT

I said to You:
Lord, crush my resentment
Chisel my rebellion
Chain my self-centeredness
Crash my inconsistency
Stifle my fears.

You said to me:
I will cleanse you with My blood
I will melt you with My Love
I will flood you with Myself
Until you grasp anew—
Our intention is the same
But the method is Mine.

RESEMBLANCE

Lord, somewhere I read
That when two people
Love deeply
When they live together
Sharing
Caring
Giving
Forgiving
Eventually they begin
To resemble each other.
Lord, how long will it be
Before I look like *You?*

WHO AM I?

(Acts 17:28)

In Him
I live
I move
I have my being.
Therefore
Who am I?
I am in God.
In the
Great *I AM*
I am.

Thank You, Lord.
At last
I know
Who I am.

WINNER

Lord
How did it happen
That You chose me
To belong to You?
Whatever the reason
One thing is certain:
I won.

WHO, ME?

Lord
All of a sudden today
You picked me up
And hugged me
And hugged me
For no discernible reason.
I was puzzled.
After all—
I hadn't picked up my toys
Or practiced my lessons
Or brought You a daisy bouquet—

Hesitantly, I asked why.
You smiled and said:
I love you, that's all.
Then You added:
I long to hug you more often.
Why don't You, Lord?
You are too busy.
Too busy, Lord?
Too busy hugging yourself.

TELL ME AGAIN, LORD,
I FORGET

I don't want to get up this morning, Lord.
The day is cold and misty
I feel it
Even with the shades drawn.
My head aches
My heart skips beats
And my fingers tingle.
I just can't handle the pressure
Piled sky-high.
Lord
Do something
Say something
I'm scared.

Little one
I've already shown you
I've already told you
If you obey
You'll see.
If you refuse
I'm so sorry.

Tell me again, Lord
I forget.

THANK YOU FOR SAYING NO

Lord, day after day I've thanked You
For saying yes.
But when have I genuinely thanked You
For saying no?

Yet I shudder to think
Of the possible smears
The cumulative blots on my life
Had You not been sufficiently wise
To say an *unalterable* no.

So thank You for saying no
When my wantlist for things
Far exceeded my longing for You.
When I asked for a stone
Foolishly certain I asked for bread.
Thank You for saying no
To my petulant "Just this time, Lord?"
Thank You for saying no
To senseless excuses
Selfish motives
Dangerous diversions.

Thank You for saying no
When the temptation that enticed me
Would have bound me beyond escape.

Thank You for saying no
When I asked You to leave me alone.

Above all
Thank You for saying no
When in anguish I asked
"If I give You all else
May I keep *this?*"

Lord, my awe increases
When I see the wisdom
Of Your divine no.

MASTER ARTIST

There are days, Lord
Frightening and mysterious
When You seem to splash across
The canvas of my heart
With wasted strokes—
Like an amateur artist
Carelessly mixing pigment.
Frankly
Your colors appear unblended
Your strokes haphazard.
Instead of design
I see blobs of distortion.
Today, Lord
This very hour
Dissolve my apprehension
Renew my confidence
Settle my conviction
That You have planned
The total design.
Finally, Lord
When the finished canvas
Is luminously displayed
Make this my song of affirmation:
The pattern is perfectly clear.

MY ONLY DEFENSE

The powerful reality grips me, Lord
That when I kneel in Your presence
To ask Your forgiveness
I am utterly stripped of facade.
You accept no big-name references
No high-caliber recommendations.
Extenuating circumstances
Crumble to dust
In Your court of appeal . . .
I am forgiven never
Because of inherited tendencies
Or emotional discomfort
Or nagging weakness . . .
I can never plead
Corrupt environment
Or life's strange twistings
Or my own unbelievable stupidity. . .
Ultimately I have one solitary defense.
Only one—
But always one:
Forgive me, God
For Jesus' sake.
Like a song unending
The words keep singing . . .
I am totally forgiven
I am continually cleansed
Just for Jesus' sake.

COURTESY

I tried to be
Very courteous.
I smiled and said
"No thank You, Lord."
You smiled back and said
"Omit the first word
And I'll be delighted
With your courtesy—
And more delighted
With your trust."
"Thank You, Lord."

TODAY, LORD

Yesterday, Lord
When You asked what I wanted
Above all else
I said I wanted to be
Exclusively Yours.
Today, as You startle me
With opportunities
Keep me from begging off
Until tomorrow.

EITHER WAY

Lord
I'm never really whole
Apart from You.
Or shall I say it
Another way:
Without You
I am only a part.

SUPERLATIVES

Lord
It's wonderful
That You see me

More wonderful
That You lead me

Most wonderful
That You love me.

Good, better, best?
No—with You
All is superlative:
Always best.

HOLD ME TO MY YES

I'm frightened, Lord
Bewildered
What shall I do?
I could have sworn I was free—
Free from the sinister temptation
So fiercely threatening me.
Months have passed
Even years
Not once have old memories haunted me
Nor has ugliness plagued me
Until now.
Suddenly
Tauntingly
Daringly
Desire steals in
Like a midnight thief.
It clutches
Crushes
Until my thoughts reel
Until my breath is tight.

Lord, the day I said *yes* to You
My total being responded.
This You know.
Now while the enemy seeks
The target of my heart
Don't let me renege—
Hold me to my yes.

For this we both know:
To sacrifice the ultimate
For the immediate
Spells disaster
Despair
Defeat.

Promises
Kept

FOOLISH CHILD

All day long
I've stumbled from
Worry to worry
When I could have soared
From prayer to prayer.
Forgive me, Lord.

THERE IS ROOM

You know how it happened, Lord:
She said, "May I live with you
Just a little while?
I have no place to go.
I'm lonely
And afraid."
I hastily glanced at the small room.
I thought of other rooms
Smaller and extremely crowded.
I said, "You see my small house.
There is really no room.
But I have room in my heart
For caring
For praying
I'll make phone calls—
There must be a family somewhere . . ."
That was this morning, Lord.
All day long
I prayed
I called
I waited . . .
Then You accomplished
What I cannot explain.
Through the hours
You pushed back the walls—
Until suddenly, tonight
There is room for her in my house
As well as in my heart
You are indeed a Master Builder!

CREATURE OF MOODS

I am a creature of incredible moods.

I read "In everything give thanks"
And I am all gung-ho.
Nothing shall cool my gratitude.
Through temptest and turmoil
Through fire and flood
I shall offer the sacrifice of praise.

And then a critical remark
Hits the target of my heart
Or I run out of gas on the freeway
Or my husband brings a dinner guest
When I have but two chops broiling
And my gratitude flutters and falls
Like an autumn leaf.

Then all at once I remember
That You did not say
"Feel thankful."
You only said
"Give thanks."
And this truth so delights me
That soon I feel thankful again!

Lord, I am indeed
A creature of incredible moods.
Or am I learning a sublime truth?

UNPREDICTABLE

Sometimes, Lord
You come up with such
Unpredictable answers—
Today
I related my predicament
I explained my desperation
I begged You
To get me out of this mess.
Your only answer:
"I beg you to let Me in on this mess."

ALL GONE

Thank You, Lord
For cleansing my heart's wound
With Living Water.
Thank You for Your bandage
Of pure, gentle love.
Thank You for the kiss of comfort.
At last the hurt is gone.

KEEP

I sit here at my desk
With Your Word before me—
A red pencil in my hand.
Suddenly the word *keep*
Looms from the page
Black and bold:
"He will *keep*
Keep
Keep
That which I have committed . . ."
Really, Lord?
This haunting anxiety?
This brick barrier which is
Blocking my peace?
This sinister intrusion?
It's so heavy, Lord
The weight of it is breaking me.
But You said You'd *keep*
So I give it to You now
Palms down.

Release!
Relief!
Laughter!
Joy!

FREE ME, LORD

Lord, just today I read
That Paul and Silas were
Stripped and beaten
With wooden whips.
"Again and again the rods
Slashed across their bared backs."
But in their desolate dungeon
Their feet clamped in stocks
They prayed
They sang
They praised.
In this musty midnight of my life
Imprisoned in a dungeon of confusion
Bound by chains of anguish
Help me, please help me
To pray
To sing
To praise
Until the foundation shakes
Until the gates fling open
Until the chains fall off
Until I am free
To share the Good News
With other chain-bound prisoners.

HIS SHEEP AM I

(2 Peter 2:22)

Lord, now that You
Have washed me
Whiter than snow
Don't let me wallow
In filth and mud again—
For I am a sheep
And not a pig.

SON-LIGHT

Lord, take away the blind spots
And give me 20-20 spiritual vision.
Let me see Your plan
This very day.
May I not be overly protective
Of my spiritual sight.
Colored glasses are fine
For sunlight
But not for Son-Light.
The more directly
I face the Son
The clearer my vision.

BEST FRIENDS

Lord
Today I read
"And Abraham believed God . . .
And he was called
The friend of God."
Please, Lord, give me
A faith so strong
That we may be
Very best friends!

TAKE OVER

At first, Lord, I asked You
To take sides with me.
With David the Psalmist
I circled and underlined:
"The Lord is for me . . ."
"Maintain my rights, O Lord . . ."
"Let me stand above my foes . . ."
But with all my pleading
I lay drenched in darkness
Until in utter confusion I cried
"Don't take sides, Lord
Just take over."
And suddenly it was morning.

UNCONDITIONAL GUARANTEE

Lord
Your promise
Is my guarantee
That all
That could
Never happen
Is happening
This very day
In me.

THIS, TOO, IS FAITH

Lord, I am desperately afraid
Of tempestuous waves.
Had I been on the ship
The day you stilled the storm
I would have been the first
To scream for help—
This I shamelessly admit.
But, Lord, this too is faith:
Boldly expecting You
To do something about it.

ROMANS 8—TO ME

God
I may fall flat on my face
I may fail until I feel
Old and beaten and done in
Yet Your love for me is changeless.
All the music may go out of my life
My private world may shatter to dust
Even so You will hold me
In the palm of Your steady hand.
No turn in the affairs
Of my fractured life
Can baffle You.
Satan with all his braggadocio
Cannot distract You.
Nothing can separate me
From Your measureless love:
Pain can't
Disappointment can't
Anguish can't.
Yesterday, today, tomorrow can't.
The loss of my dearest love can't.

Death can't.
Life can't.
Riots war insanity unidentity
Hunger neurosis disease—
None of these things
Nor all of them heaped together
Can budge the fact
That I am dearly loved.

Completely forgiven
And forever free
Through Jesus Christ
Your beloved Son.

REVERSAL

I said: Lord, look at me
Just look at me
All of life upside down—
Tangled emotions smeared with fear
Guilt
Despair
Disgust
A prisoner of myself.
The hopeless thing is that
It's all decided.
I'm defenseless
At the end of my rope
Locked in
And I've tried, Lord
Tried desperately.
But how does one see without eyes
Or walk without feet?
How, Lord?

You said: Come unto Me.
You need not cringe
Nor climb
Nor compete
Nor change
Come even without feeling
Without tokens
Without merit or hope

But come.
Come now.

I came
And all of life
Turned right side up.

SPARROW—AND ME

Oh, Lord
It's wonderful—
Just so wonderful
That You
Really do see
The sparrow
And me.

HIGH INTEREST

Lord
Since I've invested
My life in Your Kingdom
I'm amazed
At Your astronomical
Rate of interest.

LAST WORD

I read, "In everything give thanks."
I said, "Lord, I'm in deep trouble—
You know I can't thank You for this."
You said, "My word is a command
And not a suggestion, dear child."

I read, "Your sins are forgiven you."
I said, "Thank you for forgiving me—
I repeat the same sin so often."
You said, "I can deliver, as well as forgive."

I read, "Trust in the Lord at all times."
I said, "You know how earnestly I try."
You said, "My Word says Trust."

Lord, it seems to me
You always have
The last word.

LIMPING HOME

Lord
With a crooked stick for a cane
I'm limping home.
Mocked and maligned
Stooped and stupid
Soiled and shabby
I limp toward You.
You could say, "I told you so."
You could say, "It's a little too late."
You could say, "Wait while I think it over."
You could sweep me under the rug—
We both know I deserve far less.
But when I see the Cross
And the Man who died there
Suddenly I know I limp
Toward unfathomable love
And there is forgiveness
Rushing toward me.
I don't ask for a banquet, Lord
Nor do I need a gold ring.
I'm so hungry
So thirsty
For You.

Other Living Books Best-sellers

ROOM FOR ONE MORE by Nyla Booth and Ann Scott. Ann and Phil Scott, with two daughters of their own, found themselves adopting not one, but eventually fifteen needy children. A heartwarming true story. 07-5711 $3.50.

SUSANNA by Glen Williamson. Meet Susanna Wesley, the mother of John and Charles Wesley, a most unusual though lesser-known woman of Christian history. This stirring testimony will challenge Christians to establish a strong foundation of faith for their children. 07-6691 $3.50.

LORD, COULD YOU HURRY A LITTLE? by Ruth Harms Calkin. These prayer-poems from the heart of a godly woman trace the inner workings of the heart, following the rhythms of the day and the seasons of the year with expectation and love. 07-3816 $2.95.

BITTERSWEET LOVE by Betty R. Headapohl. In this touching romance, Trevor, a wealthy land developer, falls in love with Starr, a health food store owner. Then Starr's former fiancé reappears, and the sparks start to fly. 07-0181 $3.50.

HUNTED GUN by Bernard Palmer. Colorado rancher John Breck encounters an ambush, suspicious townspeople, and deceit spawned by gold fever in this fast-paced yet thoughtful western for adults. 07-1497 $3.50.

HER CONTRARY HEART by Lois T. Henderson. A fascinating historical romance revealing the inner turbulence of a young and spirited woman who questions the tenets of the strict Harmonist Society to which she belongs. 07-1401 $3.95.

SUCCESS: THE GLENN BLAND METHOD by Glenn Bland. The author shows how to set goals and make plans that really work. His ingredients of success include spiritual, financial, educational, and recreational balances. 07-6689 $3.50.

KAREN'S CHOICE by Janice Hermansen. College students Karen and Jon fall in love and are heading toward marriage when Karen discovers she is pregnant. Struggle with Karen and Jon through the choices they make and observe how they cope with the consequences and eventually find the forgiveness of Christ. 07-2027 $2.95.

LET ME BE A WOMAN by Elisabeth Elliot. In these days of conflicting demands and cultural pressures, what kind of woman do you wish to be? With profound and moving insights, this best-selling author presents her unique perspective of womanhood. 07-2162 $3.95.

RAISING CHILDREN by Linda Raney Wright. Twelve well-known Christian mothers give their views on parenthood, sharing insights and personal experiences from family life that will both amuse you and cause you to think. 07-5136 $2.95.

The books listed are available at your bookstore. If unavailable, send check with order to cover retail price plus $1.00 per book for postage and handling to:

Christian Book Service
Box 80
Wheaton, Illinois 60189

Prices and availability subject to change without notice. Allow 4–6 weeks for delivery.